TOP TEN KEYS FOR SUCCESSFUL WRITING AND PRODUCTIVITY

B Alan Bourgeois

AWARD-WINNING AUTHOR
AWARD-WINNING SPEAKER
AUTHOR ADVOCATE

PLANNING YOUR TIME HELPS WITH WRITING AND SUCCESS

Top Ten Keys for Successful Writing and Productivity

© B Alan Bourgeois 2023

All rights reserved. No part of this publication may be reproduced, stored in a retrieval system, or transmitted in any form or by any means, electronic, mechanical, photocopying, recording, or otherwise, without the prior written permission of the publisher.

The information and opinions expressed in this book are believed to be accurate and reliable, but no responsibility or liability is assumed by the publisher for any errors, omissions, or any damages caused by the use of these products, procedures, or methods presented herein.

The book is sold and distributed on an "as is" basis without warranties of any kind, either expressed or implied, including but not limited to warranties of merchantability or fitness for a particular purpose. The purchaser or reader of this book assumes complete responsibility for the use of these materials and information.

Any legal disputes arising from the use of this book shall be governed by the laws of the jurisdiction where the book was purchased, without regard to its conflict of law provisions, and shall be resolved exclusively in the courts of that jurisdiction.

ISBN: 978-1-0881-6587-4

Publisher: Bourgeois Media & Consulting (<u>BourgeoisMedia.com</u>)

Introduction

The keys you discover in this book can also be found in other titles from our Top Ten Series. This book contains a wealth of valuable information that will assist you in maintaining focus on your current manuscript. It will also provide guidance on improving time management, allowing you to complete, refine, and ultimately publish your work.

Moreover, by following the book's advice, you can seamlessly transition into marketing your manuscript from the very moment you start writing it. This is a crucial factor for achieving success and maximizing book sales.

Contents

1. <u>Write Regularly</u>: Make writing a habit and commit to a regular writing schedule.
2. <u>Set Goals</u>: Set realistic writing goals and break them down into manageable tasks.
3. <u>Manage Time Effectively:</u> Use time management techniques to make the most of your writing time.
4. <u>Focus on Quality</u>: Take the time to produce high-quality writing that meets your standards.
5. <u>Edit and Revise</u>: Edit and revise your work to improve its quality and ensure that it is polished and professional.
6. <u>Seek Feedback</u>: Get feedback from beta readers, writing groups, or editors to improve your writing.
7. <u>Build an Audience</u>: Develop a following by promoting your work

on social media and through other channels.
8. <u>Network</u>: Connect with other authors, agents, and publishers to build your professional network.
9. <u>Stay Organized</u>: Keep track of your writing projects, deadlines, and other important information to stay organized and on track.
10. <u>Stay Motivated</u>: Stay motivated by reminding yourself of why you started writing, and by celebrating your successes along the way.

1
Write Regularly

As an author, one of the most important things you can do is to write regularly. Writing is a craft, and like any craft, it requires practice to become proficient. The more you write, the better you will become at it. Here are some tips on how to make writing a habit and commit to a regular writing schedule:

1. Set a goal: Decide how much time you want to spend writing each day or week, and set a goal for yourself. Make sure your goal is achievable and realistic. For example, you might decide to write for 30 minutes every day, or for two hours every Saturday morning.
2. Find a time that works for you: Everyone has different schedules and preferences when it comes

to writing. Some people prefer to write early in the morning, while others prefer to write in the evening. Experiment with different times of day and see what works best for you.

3. Create a routine: Once you've found a time that works for you, create a routine around it. Make writing a part of your daily or weekly routine, just like eating breakfast or going for a run.

4. Minimize distractions: Distractions can be a major barrier to writing regularly. Make sure you eliminate as many distractions as possible during your designated writing time. Turn off your phone, close your email, and find a quiet place to write.

5. Use prompts: Sometimes it can be difficult to know what to write about. Using prompts can help you get started and keep your writing on track. There are many

writing prompt websites and books available, or you can simply jot down a few ideas before you start writing.
6. Don't worry about quality: When you're first starting to write regularly, don't worry too much about the quality of your writing. The most important thing is to get into the habit of writing regularly. You can always go back and revise later.
7. Track your progress: Keep track of how much time you're spending writing each day or week, and how much you're accomplishing. Seeing your progress can be a great motivator and help you stay on track.

By making writing a habit and committing to a regular writing schedule, you'll be well on your way to becoming a successful author. Remember, practice makes perfect, and the more you write, the better you'll become.

2
Set Goals

As a writer, setting goals is a crucial part of your journey. Goals give you direction, help you measure progress, and keep you motivated. But setting unrealistic goals can lead to frustration and disappointment. So, it's essential to set realistic writing goals that you can achieve.

Here are some tips to help you set realistic writing goals:

1. Define Your Writing Goals

The first step in setting writing goals is to define what you want to achieve. Do you want to finish your novel? Publish a collection of short stories? Write a screenplay? Once you know what you want to achieve, you can set goals that align with your overall vision.

2. Break Goals Down into Manageable Tasks

Once you have defined your goals, break them down into manageable tasks. For example, if your goal is to finish your novel in six months, you could break it down into smaller tasks like writing a certain number of words or pages each day or week.

3. Prioritize Your Goals

It's essential to prioritize your goals so that you focus on the most important ones first. Consider which goals will have the most significant impact on your writing career and start with those.

4. Be Realistic

When setting writing goals, it's important to be realistic. Don't set a goal to write 10,000 words a day if you know that's not feasible for you. Instead, set a goal that challenges you but is still achievable.

5. Set Deadlines

Setting deadlines can help you stay focused and motivated. Give yourself a deadline for each task you set and stick to it. Make sure your deadlines are realistic and achievable, so you don't feel overwhelmed.

6. Celebrate Your Achievements

When you achieve a writing goal, take the time to celebrate your achievement. This will help keep you motivated and focused on achieving your next goal.

7. Re-evaluate Your Goals

As you progress, you may need to re-evaluate your goals. If you find that a goal is too easy or too difficult, adjust it accordingly. It's essential to have flexible goals that you can adjust as needed.

In conclusion, setting realistic writing goals is critical to your success as a writer. By defining your goals, breaking them down into manageable tasks, prioritizing them, being realistic, setting deadlines, celebrating your achievements, and re-evaluating your goals, you can set yourself up for success. Remember that it's okay to adjust your goals as needed, and don't forget to celebrate your progress along the way!

3
Manage Time Effectively

As a writer, it's essential to manage your time effectively to make the most of your writing time. Time management can help you increase your productivity and achieve your writing goals. Here are some techniques to help you manage your time effectively:

1. Prioritize your tasks: Before you start working on your writing project, prioritize your tasks. Identify the most important tasks and complete them first. This way, you'll ensure that you're using your time efficiently and not wasting it on tasks that aren't as important.
2. Create a schedule: Create a schedule and allocate specific time slots for writing. Make sure that you stick to your schedule

and use your time productively. You can use a planner or a digital calendar to help you stay on track.
3. Eliminate distractions: Distractions can be a significant obstacle to effective time management. To eliminate distractions, turn off your phone, close unnecessary tabs on your computer, and let others know that you're not available during your scheduled writing time.
4. Break your work into manageable chunks: Breaking your work into manageable chunks can help you avoid feeling overwhelmed. Instead of trying to write an entire chapter in one sitting, break it down into smaller sections that you can complete in shorter periods.
5. Use a timer: Using a timer can help you focus on your writing and avoid distractions. Set a timer for a specific amount of

time, say 30 minutes, and work on your writing project during that time. Take a break when the timer goes off, and then repeat the process.
6. Take breaks: Taking regular breaks can help you avoid burnout and stay productive. Take a break every hour or so and do something relaxing, like going for a walk or practicing yoga.
7. Use productivity tools: There are many productivity tools available that can help you manage your time more effectively. Consider using a task manager, a writing app, or a time-tracking tool to help you stay on track and avoid distractions.

By using these technique
manage your time effecti
the most of your writing
Remember, effective ti

is key to achieving your writing goals and becoming a successful writer.

4
Focus on Quality

As an author, it's essential to focus on producing high-quality writing that meets your standards. While it may be tempting to rush through your work to meet deadlines or produce more content, taking the time to produce quality writing is key to building a loyal readership and establishing yourself as a reputable author.

Here are some tips to help you focus on quality:

1. Take breaks: It's easy to get caught up in the flow of writing, but taking breaks can help you avoid burnout and maintain a fresh perspective on your work. Taking a break can be as simple as going for a walk, meditating, or

doing something unrelated to writing for a short period.
2. Revise your work: After you've finished your first draft, take the time to revise your work thoroughly. Look for areas where you can improve the clarity, flow, and coherence of your writing. This process can be time-consuming, but it's essential for producing high-quality work.
3. Use beta readers: Beta readers are individuals who read your work and provide feedback. They can offer valuable insights into areas where your writing may be unclear or where you can improve your storytelling. Beta readers can be friends, family members, or members of writing communities.
4. Edit your work: Editing is an essential part of producing high-quality writing. After you've revised your work, take the time to edit it carefully. Look for

spelling and grammar errors, awkward phrasing, and inconsistencies in your story.
5. Hire a professional editor: If you're serious about producing high-quality writing, consider hiring a professional editor. An editor can provide feedback on your work, help you improve your writing, and ensure that your work meets industry standards.

In conclusion, producing high-quality writing takes time and effort, but it's essential for building a loyal readership and establishing yourself as a reputable author. By taking breaks, revising and editing your work thoroughly, using beta readers, and hiring a professional editor, you can ensure that your work is of the highest quality possible.

5
Edit and Revise

Editing and revising are essential steps in the writing process that can greatly improve the quality of your work. While it can be tempting to rush through these steps and get your work out into the world as quickly as possible, taking the time to edit and revise your work can make all the difference in the final product. Here are some tips for effectively editing and revising your writing:

1. Take a break: After finishing a draft, take a break from your work. This will allow you to come back to it with fresh eyes and a new perspective.
2. Focus on the big picture: Start by looking at the overall structure and organization of your work. Does the plot make sense? Are

there any plot holes or inconsistencies? Does the pacing flow well? Address these big-picture issues before moving on to smaller details.
3. Cut unnecessary words: Go through your work and look for any unnecessary words or phrases. This can include adverbs, repetitive phrases, and filler words. Cutting these can make your writing more concise and impactful.
4. Check for grammar and spelling errors: Use a grammar and spelling checker to catch any errors that you may have missed. However, be sure to double-check any suggestions made by the tool, as they may not always be accurate.
5. Read your work aloud: Reading your work aloud can help you catch any awkward phrasing or clunky sentences.

6. Get feedback: Consider getting feedback from beta readers, writing groups, or editors. They can provide valuable insights and suggestions for improving your work.
7. Repeat the process: After making revisions, repeat the editing and revising process until you're satisfied with the final product.

Remember, the goal of editing and revising is to improve the quality of your writing and ensure that it is polished and professional. By following these tips, you can take your writing to the next level and produce work that you can be proud of.

6
Seek Feedback

Editing and revising are essential steps in the writing process that can greatly improve the quality of your work. While it can be tempting to rush through these steps and get your work out into the world as quickly as possible, taking the time to edit and revise your work can make all the difference in the final product. Here are some tips for effectively editing and revising your writing:

1. Take a break: After finishing a draft, take a break from your work. This will allow you to come back to it with fresh eyes and a new perspective.
2. Focus on the big picture: Start by looking at the overall structure and organization of your work. Does the plot make sense? Are

there any plot holes or inconsistencies? Does the pacing flow well? Address these big-picture issues before moving on to smaller details.
3. Cut unnecessary words: Go through your work and look for any unnecessary words or phrases. This can include adverbs, repetitive phrases, and filler words. Cutting these can make your writing more concise and impactful.
4. Check for grammar and spelling errors: Use a grammar and spelling checker to catch any errors that you may have missed. However, be sure to double-check any suggestions made by the tool, as they may not always be accurate.
5. Read your work aloud: Reading your work aloud can help you catch any awkward phrasing or clunky sentences.

6. Get feedback: Consider getting feedback from beta readers, writing groups, or editors. They can provide valuable insights and suggestions for improving your work.
7. Repeat the process: After making revisions, repeat the editing and revising process until you're satisfied with the final product.

Remember, the goal of editing and revising is to improve the quality of your writing and ensure that it is polished and professional. By following these tips, you can take your writing to the next level and produce work that you can be proud of.

7
Build an Audience

As an author, building an audience is essential to your success. Whether you're a new writer or an experienced author, having a loyal following can help you connect with readers and promote your work effectively. Here are some tips on how to build an audience for your writing:

1. Identify your target audience: Knowing who your target audience is can help you tailor your content and marketing efforts to appeal to them. Consider factors such as age, gender, interests, and reading preferences when identifying your target audience.
2. Create a website or blog: Having a website or blog can help you showcase your work and build a

following. Make sure your website or blog is visually appealing and easy to navigate, and consider including content such as author interviews, book reviews, and writing tips to keep your audience engaged.
3. Utilize social media: Social media platforms such as Facebook, Twitter, and Instagram can help you connect with readers and promote your work. Make sure to post regularly, engage with your followers, and share content that is relevant to your audience.
4. Offer free content: Offering free content such as excerpts, short stories, or samples of your work can help entice readers and encourage them to check out your other work.
5. Attend events and conferences: Attending events and conferences such as book fairs or writing conferences can help you

connect with readers and other authors, and promote your work.
6. Collaborate with other authors: Collaborating with other authors can help you reach new audiences and promote your work to their followers. Consider hosting joint events or offering bundled promotions with other authors in your genre.
7. Offer promotions and giveaways: Offering promotions or giveaways such as discounted books or free merchandise can help encourage readers to check out your work and build a loyal following.

Building an audience takes time and effort, but by utilizing these tips and consistently promoting your work, you can connect with readers and achieve success as an author.

8
Network

Networking for writers is a crucial component of building a successful writing career. As a writer, it's important to connect with other professionals in the industry, including other authors, agents, publishers, and editors. These connections can help you gain valuable insights, advice, and opportunities that can propel your writing career forward.

Here are some tips on how to network effectively as a writer:

1. Attend writing conferences and events: Writing conferences and events are great opportunities to meet other writers and industry professionals. Look for conferences that focus on your genre or area of interest, and come prepared with business cards and a pitch for your work.

2. Join writing groups: Writing groups can provide valuable feedback on your work and offer opportunities to network with other writers. Look for local writing groups in your area or join online writing communities.
3. Follow and engage with industry professionals on social media: Follow agents, editors, and publishers on social media and engage with their content by commenting and sharing. This can help you establish a connection and get on their radar.
4. Be professional and courteous: When networking, always be professional and courteous. Be respectful of others' time and boundaries, and avoid coming across as pushy or entitled.
5. Offer value: When connecting with other professionals, think about what value you can offer them. Maybe you can promote their work on your social media

channels, or offer to beta read their manuscript. By offering value, you can establish yourself as a valuable contact in the industry.
6. Keep in touch: After networking with someone, be sure to follow up and keep in touch. Send a thank you note or email, and stay on their radar by sending occasional updates on your writing progress.

By networking effectively, you can build a strong professional network that can help you succeed as a writer. Remember to always be professional, courteous, and offer value, and you'll be on your way to building a successful writing career.

9
Stay Organized

As a writer, it's essential to keep track of your writing projects, deadlines, and other important information to stay organized and on track. Being organized not only helps you stay focused and productive, but it can also reduce stress and ensure that you meet your goals and deadlines.

Here are some tips to help you stay organized as a writer:

1. Use a planner or calendar: One of the most important things you can do to stay organized is to use a planner or calendar to keep track of your writing projects and deadlines. You can use a paper planner, an electronic calendar, or a combination of both.

2. Set deadlines: It's important to set deadlines for yourself to help you stay on track. When you set deadlines, make sure they are realistic and achievable.
3. Break down larger projects into smaller tasks: If you have a larger writing project, break it down into smaller tasks or milestones. This will help you stay focused and make progress towards your goal.
4. Prioritize your tasks: When you have multiple writing projects or tasks to complete, it's important to prioritize them based on their importance and deadlines. This will help you focus on the most important tasks first.
5. Create a writing schedule: Establishing a regular writing schedule can help you stay on track and make progress towards your writing goals. Set aside a specific time each day or week for writing and stick to it.

6. Use writing tools and software: There are many writing tools and software programs available that can help you stay organized and productive. These tools can include word processors, outlining software, and project management tools.
7. Keep your writing space organized: Make sure your writing space is organized and clutter-free. This will help you stay focused and avoid distractions.
8. Backup your work: Always backup your writing projects and files to ensure that you don't lose any important work. Consider using cloud-based storage or an external hard drive to keep your work safe.

By staying organized and on top of your writing projects, you can improve your productivity and increase your chances of success as a writer. Use these tips to help you stay organized and achieve your writing goals.

10
Stay Motivated

Writing is a rewarding but challenging activity that can sometimes be discouraging, particularly when faced with writer's block or lack of motivation. However, it's crucial to stay motivated if you want to succeed as a writer. Here are some tips to help you stay motivated on your writing journey.

Remind yourself of why you started writing: Whenever you feel unmotivated, take a moment to reflect on why you started writing in the first place. Did you want to share your story with the world? Did you have a message you wanted to convey? Did you enjoy the process of writing? Reconnecting with your reasons for writing can help reignite your passion for it.

Celebrate small successes: Writing can be a slow process, and it's easy to get caught up in the long-term goals, such as finishing a novel or getting published. However, celebrating small successes along the way can help keep you motivated. Did you complete a particularly challenging chapter? Did you write for a certain amount of time without distractions? Celebrate these milestones to keep your motivation high.

Create a supportive environment: Surrounding yourself with supportive people can help you stay motivated. Joining a writing group, attending conferences or workshops, or connecting with other writers online can provide you with the support and encouragement you need to keep going.

Establish a routine: Having a writing routine can help you stay motivated by making writing a regular habit. Whether you prefer to write in the morning, at night, or during your lunch break, establish a routine that works for you and stick to it.

Take breaks: Taking breaks can help you recharge your batteries and prevent burnout. Don't feel guilty about taking some time away from your writing to do something else that you enjoy.

Stay inspired: Reading books, watching movies, and exploring new places can provide inspiration for your writing. Exposing yourself to different ideas and experiences can help you stay motivated and bring fresh perspectives to your writing.

In conclusion, staying motivated as a writer is essential to achieving your writing goals. By reminding yourself of why you started writing, celebrating small successes, creating a supportive environment, establishing a routine, taking breaks, and staying inspired, you can stay motivated on your writing journey. Remember that writing is a process, and it's okay to experience setbacks and challenges along the way. Keep pushing forward, and you will achieve success as a writer.

B Alan Bourgeois began his writing career at the age of 12, writing screenplays for the Adam-12 show. Despite not submitting them for review, this experience sparked his passion for writing. However, he followed the advice of his generation and pursued higher education to secure a stable job. It wasn't until 1989, after taking a writing class at a community college, that Bourgeois wrote a short story that was published. Since then, he has written over 48 short stories and published more than 10 books, including the award-winning spiritual thriller "Extinguishing the Light."

Bourgeois has become a champion for authors and founded the Texas Authors Association in 2011 to help Texas authors better market and sell their books. This led to the creation of the Texas Authors Institute of History, Inc., and the first online museum of its kind, the Texas Authors Institute. He also created several short story contests and fundraising programs for Texas students and consolidated small-town book festivals into the Lone Star Festival, promoting Texas authors, musicians, artists, and filmmakers. In 2016, he founded the Authors Marketing Event and added a Certification program in 2017, allowing attendees to gain accreditation for their hard work in learning book marketing. His recent focus has been on assisting authors of all levels to become successful Authorpreneurs through the Authors School of Business, which offers programs to help grow their careers. He is currently working with NFTs for authors to help them increase their income channels.

Click here to schedule a FREE 15 min consultation

Click here for a more detailed biography of Alan

Click here for Testimonials

Top Ten Book Series and Other Books by the Author

Available at Your Favorite Bookstore

100+ Questions a Writer/Author Should Ask

Looking to take your writing career to the next level? Look no further than "100+ Questions a Writer/Author Should Ask"! With over 100 questions curated by Award-Winning Author & Speaker B Alan Bourgeois, the founder and CEO of the Authors School of Business, this book is a must-have for any aspiring or established writer. Bourgeois, a seasoned publisher, author advocate, and educator, brings his wealth of experience to the table to help you better understand the publishing world and succeed in your career. Don't miss out on this valuable resource.

Top Ten Mistakes Authors Make when Creating a Book Cover

Your book cover is your first impression. Don't let a lackluster design hold you back. "Top Ten Mistakes Authors Make When Creating a Book Cover" is your comprehensive guide to avoid common pitfalls and create a cover that truly represents your work. Discover practical tips on how to choose the right colors, fonts, and design, and avoid using low-quality images and cluttered layouts. With real-world examples and expert advice, this book will help you create a cover that grabs readers' attention and leads to more sales.

Don't let a poorly designed book cover hold you back from success. Whether you're self-publishing or working with a traditional publisher, "Top Ten Mistakes Authors Make When Creating a Book

Cover" is a must-read. Order your copy today and take your book to the next level!

Top Ten Things to Consider for a Great Sales Pitch

Are you struggling to create a sales pitch that really resonates with your audience? Look no further than "Top Ten Things to Consider for a Great Sales Pitch"! This ultimate guide will take you through the ten most important steps to creating a sales pitch that will grab your target audience's attention and convince them to buy your book.

Learn how to identify your target audience and highlight the unique value of your book, using emotional language to connect with readers on a personal level. Be concise and to the point, and practice your pitch until you can deliver it smoothly and confidently. Incorporate social proof and visuals to make your pitch more compelling, and tailor it to the specific interests and needs of your audience.

Above all, be authentic and genuine. With the help of "Top Ten Things to Consider for a Great Sales Pitch", you'll be able to create a sales pitch that not only sells your book, but also connects with your audience and builds a loyal fan base. Don't miss out on this essential resource for any author looking to take their sales pitch to the next level!

Top Ten Publishing Issues Authors Deal With

Are you an aspiring author struggling with the daunting publishing process? Look no further than "Top Ten Publishing Issues Authors Deal With." This essential guide tackles the most common challenges writers face, including rejection, editing, marketing, distribution, audience building, time management, and legal issues like copyright infringement. Our expert advice will help you navigate the complex world of publishing and achieve success. Plus, we'll guide you through the formatting process, even for ebooks that need to work on multiple devices and software. Don't let self-doubt and imposter syndrome hinder your progress - get the knowledge you need to thrive in the publishing world. Order your copy of "Top Ten Publishing Issues Authors Deal With" today.

Top Ten Marketing Materials an Author Should Use

"Top Ten Marketing Items Authors Should Use" is the ultimate guide for authors who want to boost book sales and increase visibility. Discover the top ten marketing materials every author should use, including eye-catching bookmarks, business cards, posters, and book trailers. You'll also learn insider tips on how to write an attention-grabbing press release and build an author website that attracts readers and media attention. Plus, social media marketing, author blogging, email newsletters, and swag creation strategies will help you connect with readers, build your author brand, and create a loyal fan base. Don't let your book languish in obscurity - get your copy of "Top Ten Marketing Items Authors Should Use" today and take the first step towards successful book promotion!

Top Ten Mistakes an Author Makes Marketing Their Books

Are you an author struggling to make a name for yourself in the crowded world of book marketing? Do you want to avoid the most common mistakes that authors make when promoting their books? Then look no further than "Top 10 Mistakes Authors Make Marketing Their Books" by B Alan Bourgeois.

As an award-winning author and author advocate with years of experience in the publishing industry, Bourgeois has seen it all when it comes to book marketing. In this insightful guide, he shares the top 10 mistakes that authors make and provides practical advice on how to avoid them.

Whether you're a first-time author or a seasoned pro, "Top 10 Mistakes Authors Make Marketing Their Books" is the essential guide for taking your book marketing to the next level. With Bourgeois's expert guidance, you'll learn how to identify your target audience, build a strong online presence, engage with readers, and leverage book reviews to increase sales.

Don't let common marketing mistakes hold you back from the success you deserve. Get your copy of "Top 10 Mistakes Authors Make Marketing Their Books" today and start marketing your book like a pro!

Top Ten Mistakes Authors Make During an Interview

Are you tired of stumbling through interviews, leaving the audience uninterested and disengaged? Do you struggle with staying focused and concise when answering tough questions? Look no further!

Our book provides you with the top ten mistakes authors commonly make at interviews and gives you practical tips on how to avoid them. From preparing adequately by researching the interviewer and their audience, to staying authentic and avoiding complex jargon, we cover it all.

Don't let your lack of enthusiasm or defensiveness turn off your audience. Instead, learn how to show genuine interest in your topic and stay calm during challenging questions. And most importantly, don't forget to thank your interviewer and audience for their time and attention - it can make all the difference in leaving a positive impression.

So, are you ready to improve your interview skills and leave a lasting impact on your audience? Get your copy of "Top Ten Mistakes Authors Do at Interviews" today!

Top Ten Mistakes Authors Make Presenting at Events

Are you an author struggling to present at events? "Top Ten Mistakes Authors Make Presenting at Events" is here to help you avoid common pitfalls and present your best self. Learn how to tailor your presentation to the audience's needs, engage with them effectively, promote your book without being pushy, and more!

With this ultimate guide, you'll avoid going off-topic, losing your audience's attention, and being dull and uninteresting. Practice and rehearse your presentation to deliver it smoothly and confidently. Get your copy of "Top Ten Mistakes Authors Make Presenting at Events" today and make the most of every event you attend!

Top Ten AI Programs Apps Authors Should Use

Attention all writers and authors! Are you looking for ways to improve your writing, stay organized, and streamline your workflow? Look no further than our latest book "Top Ten AI programs/Apps a writer/author should use". In this book, we have compiled a list of the top ten AI programs and apps that will help you with your writing, marketing, and workflow. From Grammarly and ProWritingAid to Hemingway and Dragon Dictation, these programs will help you write a great book.

Although the author has not used all of the programs listed, this list was compiled in 2023 from various sources and provides valuable insight into the most effective AI tools for writers and authors. Keep in mind that the AI community is constantly developing new resources and programs, so this list may not be the most up-to-date.

Don't miss out on the opportunity to improve your writing and streamline your workflow. Order "Top Ten AI programs/Apps a writer/author should use" now and start using these powerful tools to produce your best work.

Top Ten Advantages Indie Authors Have Over Traditional Authors

B Alan Bourgeois
AWARD-WINNING AUTHOR
AWARD-WINNING, SHEAKED
AUTHOR ADVOCATE

EMBRACE YOUR
FINANCIAL
RECOURSES & GIFTS

"Top Ten Advantages Indie Authors Have over Traditional" is the ultimate guide for authors looking to take control of their publishing process. With complete control over everything from writing to distribution, independent authors have more flexibility and creative control over their work.

This book highlights the benefits of indie publishing, including higher royalties, faster publishing timelines, the ability to target niche markets, and global distribution through online retailers. If you want more control over your book's content and the ability to reach readers worldwide, "Top Ten Advantages Indie Authors Have over Traditional" is a must-read. Get your copy today and start your journey towards independent publishing success!

Top Ten Pieces of Advice from an Author Advocate & Consultant

"Top Ten Pieces of Advice from an Author Advocate & Consultant" is the ultimate guide for aspiring writers. Learn from an experienced author consultant and advocate and take your writing career to the next level. From building an author platform to developing a marketing plan, this book offers invaluable insights and practical tips to help you achieve your writing goals and make your work stand out. Start your journey to becoming a successful author today by purchasing this must-have resource.

Top Twelve Things to Make the Year of the Indie Authors Great

Are you an indie author looking to make 2024 a great year for your writing career? Then look no further than the book "Top Twelve Things to Make the Year of the Indie Authors Great." This book offers valuable insights into the top 12 things that could make 2024 a great year for indie authors to gain more readers.

With increased acceptance of self-publishing and better distribution channels, indie authors have more options than ever before to reach a wider audience. Additionally, the rise of social media platforms and digital marketing offers affordable ways for authors to connect with readers and promote their work.

But that's not all. The book also covers the importance of collaborating with other authors, the increasing popularity of audiobooks, and the need for more diverse representation in literature. And for those looking to improve their writing skills and production quality, the book offers insights into the better tools and resources available to indie authors.

Finally, the book covers opportunities for indie authors to engage with their readers, showcase their work at book festivals and online events, and collaborate with traditional publishers. In short, "Top Twelve Things to Make the Year of the Indie Authors Great" is a must-read for any indie author looking to take their writing career to the next level in 2024.

Top Ten Steps for a Writers Self-Care

Writing can be an exciting and fulfilling pursuit, but it can also be stressful and overwhelming. As an author, it's important to prioritize your mental and physical health to avoid burnout and ensure longevity in your career. The Writer's Self-Care Handbook provides a comprehensive guide to help you balance your work and personal life, manage stress, and prioritize your well-being.

In this book, you'll discover practical tips and strategies for taking breaks, practicing mindfulness, setting boundaries, staying organized, connecting with others, taking care of your physical health, practicing self-compassion, finding healthy ways to manage stress, taking time for hobbies, and seeking support when needed.

Whether you're a seasoned author or just starting out, The Writer's Self-Care Handbook offers valuable insights and advice to help you thrive in your writing career while taking care of yourself. Take the first step towards a healthier, happier writing life by getting your copy today!

Top Ten Steps to Finding the Right Editor

Are you struggling to find the right editor for your writing project? Look no further than "The Author's Guide to Finding and Working with the Right Editor." In this comprehensive guide, we provide the top ten things authors should keep in mind when finding and working with an editor. From determining your editing needs to maintaining a positive relationship with your editor, this guide covers everything you need to know to ensure a successful collaboration. Learn how to research potential editors, check their credentials, communicate clearly, be open to feedback, and more. Whether you're a first-time author or a seasoned pro, this guide is essential for anyone looking to take their writing to the next level with the help of a skilled and trusted editor.

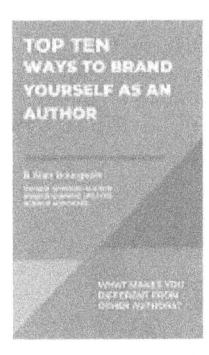

Top Ten Ways to Brand Yourself as an Author

As an author, it's not just enough to write an amazing book. In today's crowded marketplace, building a brand is essential to stand out and make a lasting impression on readers. In "Brand Yourself as an Author," we provide a top ten guide to help you define your brand identity, create a unique logo, develop a consistent visual identity, build a professional website, use social media to promote your brand, create valuable content, leverage email marketing, collaborate with other authors and brands, participate in events and conferences, and stay true to your brand. With our actionable tips, you'll learn how to build a strong and recognizable brand that resonates with your audience and sets you apart in the competitive world of publishing. Don't miss out on this essential guide to building your author brand!

Top Ten Keys for Successful Writing and Productivity

Are you an aspiring writer struggling to make writing a regular habit? Do you need help setting realistic goals and managing your time effectively to achieve success as an author? Look no further than "The Successful Author's Guide to Writing and Productivity." This comprehensive guide offers practical tips on making writing a habit, setting achievable goals, managing your time, focusing on quality, editing and revising, seeking feedback, building an audience, networking, staying organized, and staying motivated. With advice from successful authors, editors, and writing coaches, this book is a must-have for anyone looking to achieve success as an author. Whether you're a new writer or an experienced author looking to take your writing to the next level, "The

Successful Author's Guide to Writing and Productivity" will provide you with the tools and techniques you need to achieve your writing goals. Don't wait any longer to become the successful author you've always wanted to be - grab a copy of "The Successful Author's Guide to Writing and Productivity" today!

Top Ten Keys to the Business of Writing

Are you an aspiring or established author struggling with the business side of publishing? Look no further than The Business of Writing: A Comprehensive Guide for Authors. This essential guide provides in-depth information on the top ten items that every author needs to understand, from publishing contracts to managing finances. Learn how to negotiate contract terms, calculate royalties, promote and market your book, build an author platform, and understand copyright laws and intellectual property. You'll also gain insights into the publishing industry, professional networking, and ongoing professional development. With practical advice and expert insights, The Business of Writing is the ultimate resource for authors who want to succeed in the competitive world of publishing.

Top Ten Steps to Research Like a Pro

Writing a book can be a daunting task, but conducting research to support your writing can be just as challenging. With "Research Like a Pro: The Ultimate Guide for Writers," you'll learn how to conduct research like a pro, from identifying your research needs to analyzing your findings.

This book provides practical tips on how to use reliable sources, develop a research plan, and organize your materials effectively. You'll learn how to take detailed notes, keep track of citations, and analyze your research to identify patterns and themes.

With "Research Like a Pro," you'll be equipped with the knowledge and tools to effectively use research to support your writing. Whether you're a new writer or a seasoned pro, this book will help you take your research skills to the next level and produce high-quality writing that is well-supported and grounded in evidence.

Top Ten Steps to Market Mastery for Authors

Introducing "Top Ten Steps to Market Mastery for Authors." This comprehensive guide is the key to successfully publishing your book and achieving commercial success. It goes beyond simply writing a book and equips you with the essential knowledge and tools to understand and captivate your target market.

From conducting thorough market research to analyzing sales data, "Market Mastery" covers it all. Discover how to leverage social media effectively, connect with readers at book fairs and conferences, and gain valuable insights through writing groups. Stay ahead of industry trends and developments to keep your book relevant and appealing to your audience.

No matter if you're a first-time author or a seasoned pro, "Market Mastery" will empower you to identify your target audience, understand their preferences, and distinguish your book from competitors. With a strategic marketing approach and willingness to adapt, you'll be on the path to commercial success. Get ready to conquer your target audience and take your writing career to new heights with "Market Mastery."

Authors' Revolution Workbook

Welcome to the Speakers Companion Workbook. This workbook is a continuous transforming workbook to help Authors better understand the cost of being an Author in today's publishing world.

The author will review all the hidden cost of being a published author in todays world. In addition, he reviews a variety of companies and organizations that are available to help an author succeed.

The initial workbook in the form of an eBook is free to anyone who attends one of my speaking engagements. Updates can be purchased through my website at http://BourgeoisMedia.com . We encourage Authors to submit information and updates to us so that

we can continue to create a healthy and positive revolution that brings more financial security to each author who wants to earn their fair share from the works they have created. You may submit your comments and praise to us directly via email at
BourgeoisMedia@outlook.com

8TH ANNUAL AUTHORS MARKETING EVENT

TWO DAYS OF LIVE SEMINARS IN MARKETING FOR AUTHORS

SEPTEMBER 15-17

2023

The only organization that certifies authors in marketing

20 PLUS SESSIONS

AUSTIN, TEXAS

Helping Authors Since 2011

Earn your Certification at the event, or virtually at
http://AuthorsSchoolofBusiness.com

ASB is the first and only organization to offer certification in book marketing.

Join us—Why? Simple, NO ONE Does What We Do!

Three Kinds of Self-publishing Author

> **1. The Self-Publishers**
>
> **2. The Indie Authors**
>
> **3. The Authorpreneurs**

Authors School of Business is the only One-Stop program that helps authors from Pre-Publishing, Publishing, Marketing and Sales. Each program is

$14.95 per month, or get two free months when paid annual dues $149.50 in full.

Beginners

Tailored for aspiring writers who dream of becoming published authors, our program is designed to help them grow with confidence and understanding about the publishing world. We provide the knowledge and tools to position their book in a more successful position for publication and marketing, empowering them to achieve their publishing goals.

Intermediate

Tailored for published authors who are looking to gain a deep understanding of book marketing concepts and get involved in festivals, events, and other programs to promote their book, this program is designed to give them that extra edge in their book promotion efforts.

Advanced

The purpose of this program is to assist published authors in gaining a deeper understanding of advanced book marketing techniques. It is tailored for authors who are already published and are looking to enhance their marketing strategies to achieve greater success. The program offers advanced modules and concepts to empower authors with the knowledge and tools needed to excel in their book marketing efforts.

Following is everything that our Basic subscription service includes. Notices of new and exciting events that we create to help you market and sell your books are shared with subscribers as they become available.

- Participation in the DEAR Texas/DEAR Indie events – Book Festivals, Library Conferences, etc.

- ASB Author Showcase Interview - No Less the two times in a calendar year. The show is recorded live and then distributed as an audio podcast on most systems, including iHeart Radio. Video recordings are on Amazon Fire TV and YouTube. An additional marketing package authors can use on their social media system is available.

- Access to the Subscribers Only section of this website which contains articles, links, and connections to a variety of items and services to help you grow in marketing and selling your books.

- Access to all previous AME videos through our on-line campus. (40+

videos for beginners, intermediate and advanced authors.
- Discount on the Authors Marketing Event registration – an annual event held in September each year where authors and professionals join together to share valuable knowledge and insights on how to better market and sell books.

- Major discounts with our sponsors and other related industry businesses and organizations to help you save money.

- Access to our YouTube channel to promote interviews, readings, etc., of you and your books

- Newsletters with the latest information with informative articles to help you succeed

- Retail Store that includes images of book covers, and other related items from Authors on clothing, promotional items, that an author can sell or purchase. Students of ASB pay NO Set Up Fee to have their merchandise in the store, plus they earn up to 80% of the sale.

- Listing and ability to sell your book(s), and NFTs on our bookstore website http://B4R.Store

This information contained within is subject to change without notice. (Last Updated 05-0123) *ASB Prices subject to change without notice.

Printed in June 2023
by Rotomail Italia S.p.A., Vignate (MI) - Italy